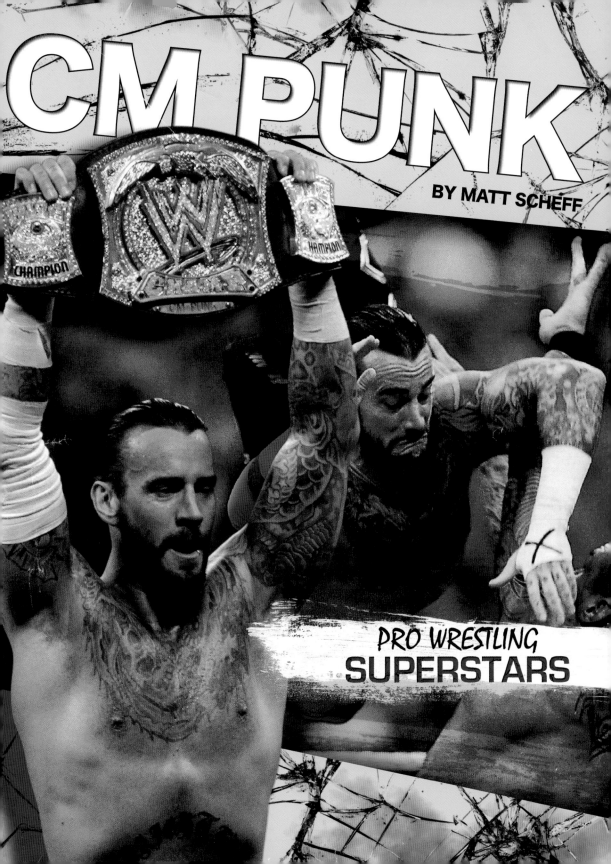

CM PUNK

BY MATT SCHEFF

PRO WRESTLING
SUPERSTARS

Published by ABDO Publishing Company, PO Box 398166, Minneapolis, MN 55439. Copyright © 2014 by Abdo Consulting Group, Inc. International copyrights reserved in all countries. No part of this book may be reproduced in any form without written permission from the publisher. SportsZone™ is a trademark and logo of ABDO Publishing Company.

Printed in the United States of America,
North Mankato, Minnesota
082013
012014

 THIS BOOK CONTAINS AT LEAST 10% RECYCLED MATERIALS.

Editor: Chrös McDougall
Series Designer: Jake Nordby

Photo Credits: Jim R. Bounds/AP Images for WWE, cover, 1, 6-7, 10-11, 28-29, 30 (top), 31; Paul Abell/AP Images, cover (background), 1 (background), 14, 30 (bottom); Zuma Press/Icon SMI, 4-5, 15, 18, 19, 22-23; SI1 WENN Photos/Newscom, 8, 9; Matt Roberts/Zuma Press/Icon SMI, 12-13, 16-17, 20-21; Mike Lano Photojournalism, 24-25, 30 (middle); SI1 WENN Photos/Newscom, 25; Mel Evans/AP Images, 26-27

Library of Congress Control Number: 2013945878

Cataloging-in-Publication Data

Scheff, Matt.
  CM Punk / Matt Scheff.
    p. cm. -- (Pro wrestling superstars)
Includes index.
ISBN 978-1-62403-135-9
1. CM Punk, 1978- --Juvenile literature. 2. Wrestlers--United States--Biography--Juvenile literature. 1. Title.
796.812092--dc23
[B]

2013945878

Contents

CM Punk goes after Chris Jericho at WrestleMania 28.

RIVALRY
MATCH

The crowd roared as World Wrestling Entertainment (WWE) champion CM Punk walked to the ring. It was Extreme Rules 2012. Punk was taking on his biggest rival, Chris Jericho.

It was a tough match. The wrestlers battled back and forth. Jericho appeared ready to finish Punk off. But Punk escaped. Then Punk threw Jericho into the corner. He lifted Jericho to begin his finishing move, the GTS ("Go to Sleep"). Punk lifted his knee and dropped Jericho's face onto it. It was lights out for Jericho. Punk was still the champion.

MEET PHILLIP JACK BROOKS

CM Punk's real name is Phillip Jack Brooks. He was born October 26, 1978, in Chicago, Illinois. Brooks had a tough childhood. His family didn't have much money. What little money they had his parents often spent on cigarettes and alcohol. Brooks said his dad was an alcoholic.

Brooks turned to punk rock music to escape hard times. He loved the band Minor Threat. The band told fans to live a "straight edge" lifestyle. That meant no drugs, alcohol, or tobacco. Brooks loved the message and vowed to be a straight edge.

FAST FACT

Punk has a tattoo on his stomach that reads "straight edge."

Mark Henry crushes Punk during a 2011 match.

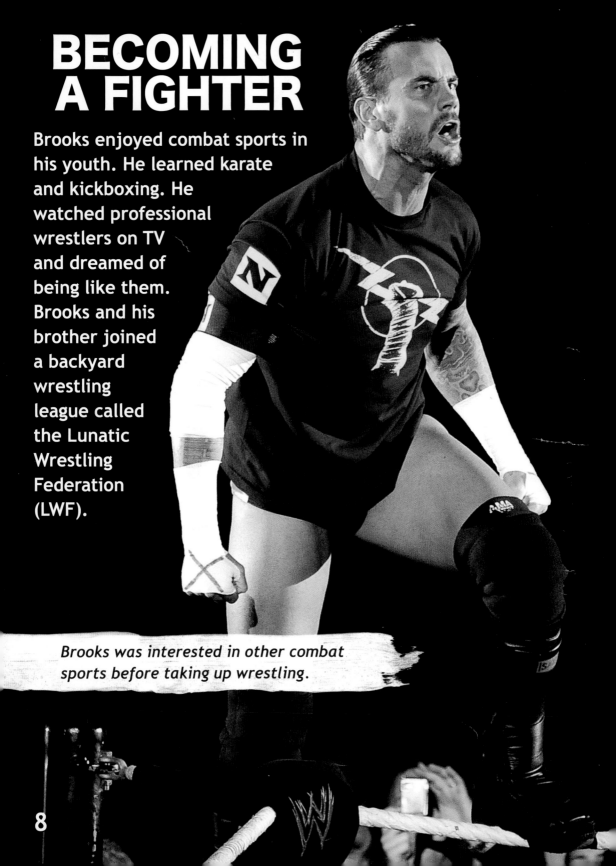

BECOMING A FIGHTER

Brooks enjoyed combat sports in his youth. He learned karate and kickboxing. He watched professional wrestlers on TV and dreamed of being like them. Brooks and his brother joined a backyard wrestling league called the Lunatic Wrestling Federation (LWF).

Brooks was interested in other combat sports before taking up wrestling.

Punk gets ready to lay a big move on Alberto Del Rio.

9

Punk stands on Big Show's shoulders to prepare for a move in a tag-team match against the Miz and John Cena.

FAST FACT

Punk is an expert at the martial art of Muay Thai. In Muay Thai, fighters use all parts of their bodies as weapons.

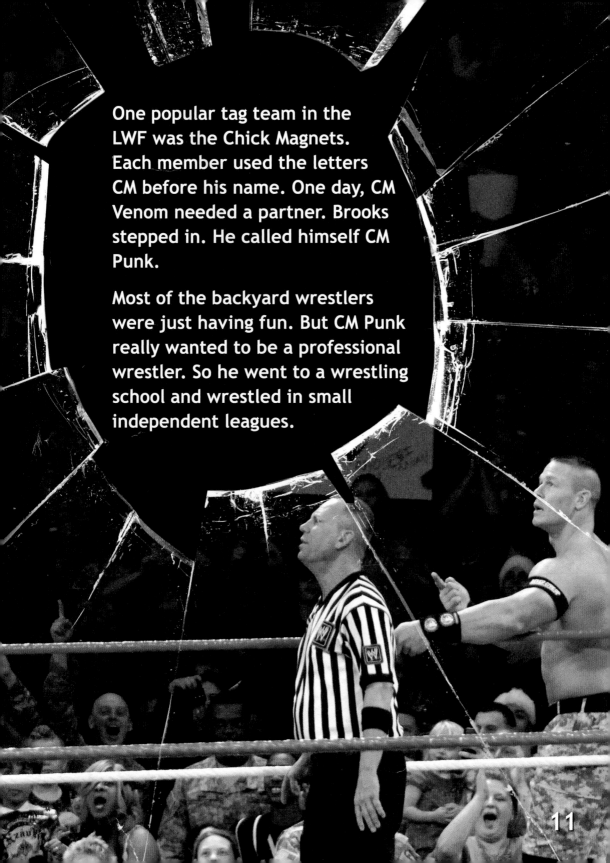

One popular tag team in the LWF was the Chick Magnets. Each member used the letters CM before his name. One day, CM Venom needed a partner. Brooks stepped in. He called himself CM Punk.

Most of the backyard wrestlers were just having fun. But CM Punk really wanted to be a professional wrestler. So he went to a wrestling school and wrestled in small independent leagues.

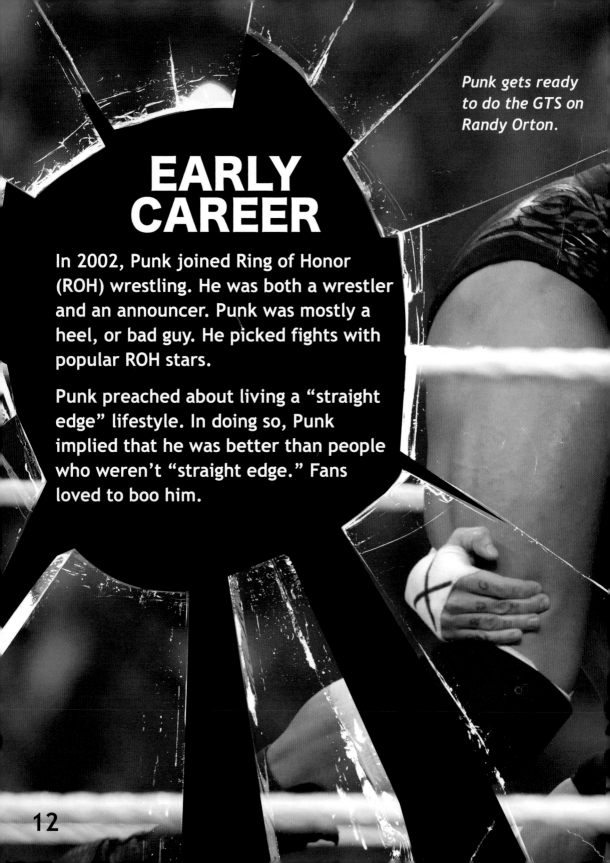

Punk gets ready to do the GTS on Randy Orton.

EARLY CAREER

In 2002, Punk joined Ring of Honor (ROH) wrestling. He was both a wrestler and an announcer. Punk was mostly a heel, or bad guy. He picked fights with popular ROH stars.

Punk preached about living a "straight edge" lifestyle. In doing so, Punk implied that he was better than people who weren't "straight edge." Fans loved to boo him.

FAST FACT

Punk and partner Colt Cabana formed the tag team Second City Saints. They won the ROH tag-team championship twice. Ace Steel was sometimes in the Second City Saints, too.

Punk dives off the ropes at Randy Orton during WrestleMania 27.

CM Punk's reputation was growing. In June 2005, he won the ROH world championship. But he didn't stay to enjoy his title. Punk signed with WWE. He was not ready for the big shows yet, however. WWE wanted him to practice more and become a better wrestler. So Punk went to Ohio Valley Wrestling (OVW) to get experience. He won his first title belt there after just two months!

Punk at WrestleMania 28

15

Punk, right, *battles Christian during a Money in the Bank match at WrestleMania 25.*

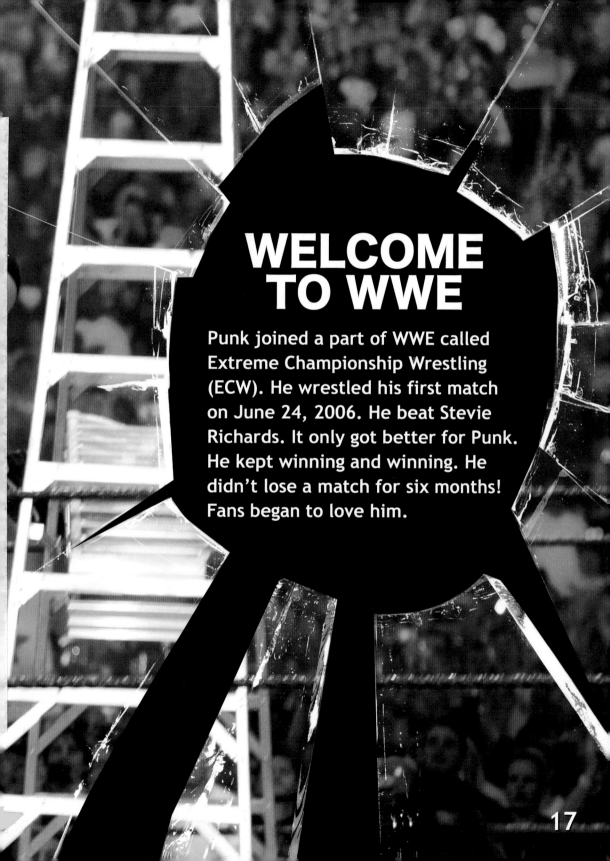

WELCOME TO WWE

Punk joined a part of WWE called Extreme Championship Wrestling (ECW). He wrestled his first match on June 24, 2006. He beat Stevie Richards. It only got better for Punk. He kept winning and winning. He didn't lose a match for six months! Fans began to love him.

17

Punk beats up on Chris Jericho at WrestleMania 28.

Punk set his sights on the ECW championship. He failed in his first several tries to win the belt. But he finally won it in September 2007. He pinned the champion, John Morrison, after a GTS. After the match, Punk fell to his knees and celebrated with the screaming fans.

Punk climbs the ropes to give the crowd a good look at his title belt.

Punk soon became known for another kind of match. He dominated the WWE's Money in the Bank matches. In these matches, eight wrestlers battle to climb a ladder in the middle of the ring and grab a briefcase hanging from the ceiling. Punk won the Money in the Bank in 2008 and again in 2009. No other wrestler has ever won two times in a row.

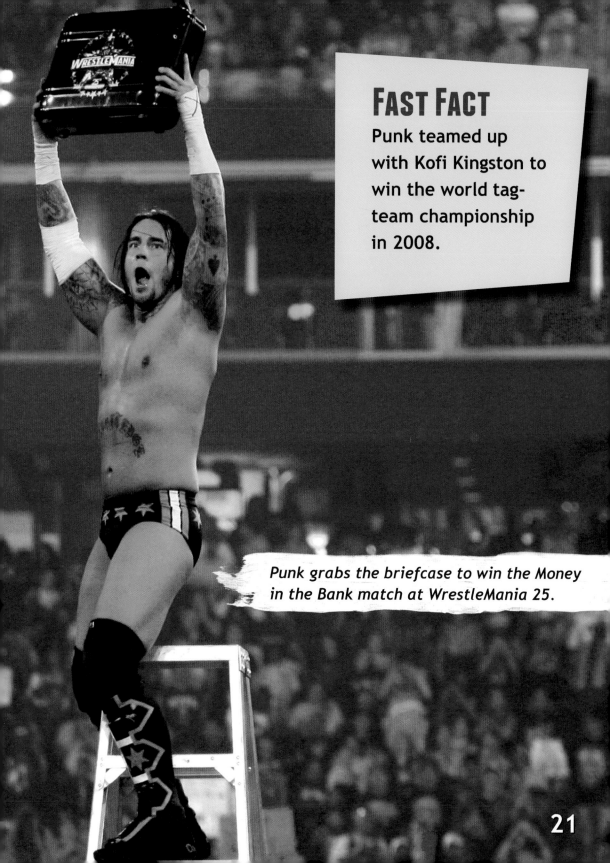

Punk grabs the briefcase to win the Money in the Bank match at WrestleMania 25.

Punk shows off his title belt at WrestleMania 28.

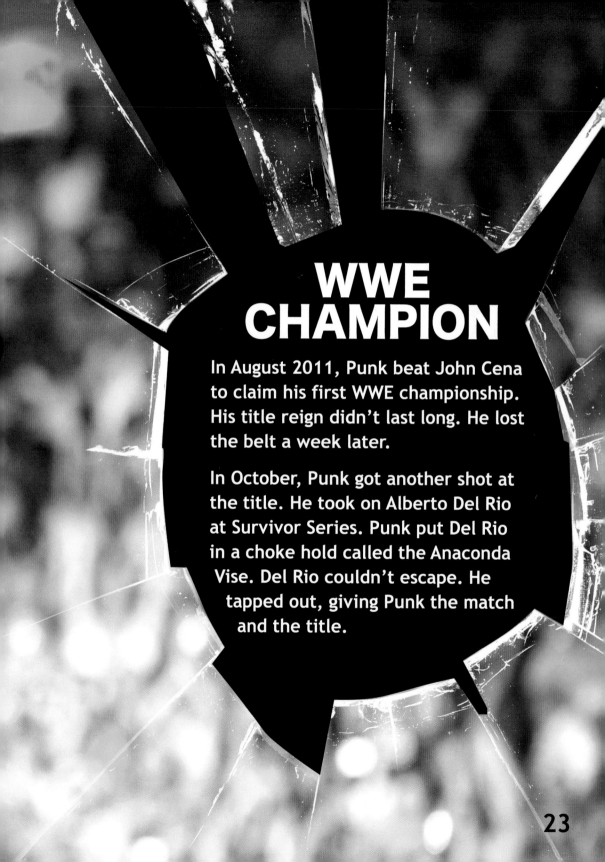

WWE CHAMPION

In August 2011, Punk beat John Cena to claim his first WWE championship. His title reign didn't last long. He lost the belt a week later.

In October, Punk got another shot at the title. He took on Alberto Del Rio at Survivor Series. Punk put Del Rio in a choke hold called the Anaconda Vise. Del Rio couldn't escape. He tapped out, giving Punk the match and the title.

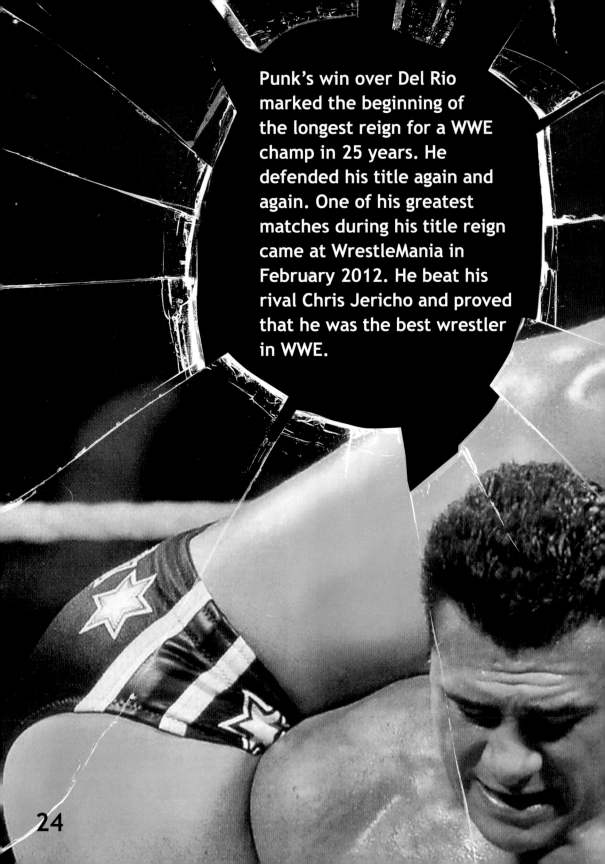

Punk's win over Del Rio marked the beginning of the longest reign for a WWE champ in 25 years. He defended his title again and again. One of his greatest matches during his title reign came at WrestleMania in February 2012. He beat his rival Chris Jericho and proved that he was the best wrestler in WWE.

Punk battles Alberto Del Rio.

Punk celebrates in 2012.

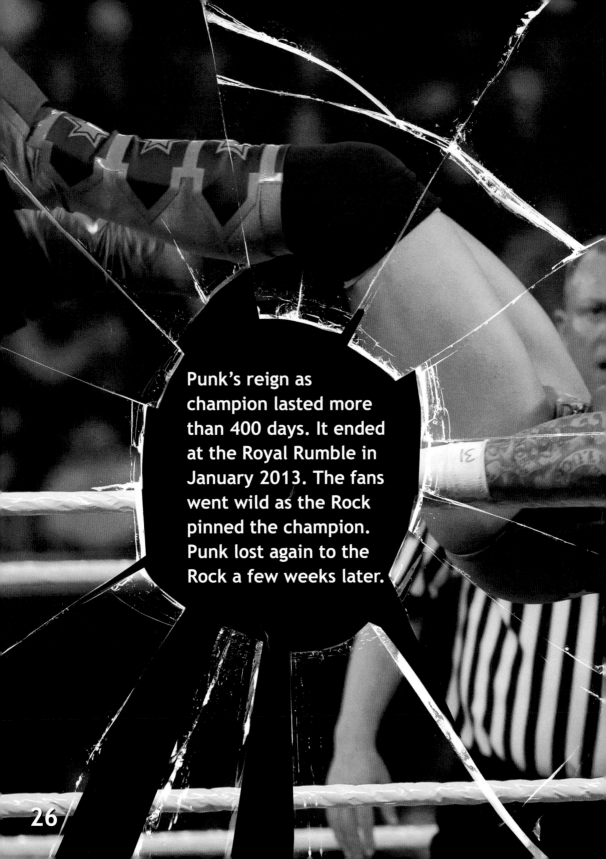

Punk's reign as champion lasted more than 400 days. It ended at the Royal Rumble in January 2013. The fans went wild as the Rock pinned the champion. Punk lost again to the Rock a few weeks later.

The Undertaker hits Punk during WrestleMania in 2013.

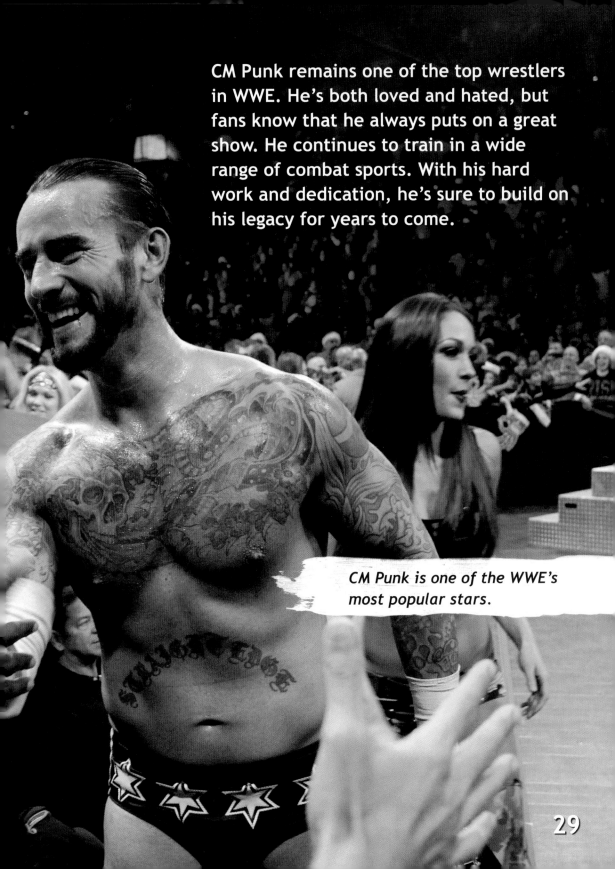

CM Punk remains one of the top wrestlers in WWE. He's both loved and hated, but fans know that he always puts on a great show. He continues to train in a wide range of combat sports. With his hard work and dedication, he's sure to build on his legacy for years to come.

CM Punk is one of the WWE's most popular stars.

TIMELINE

1978
Phillip Jack Brooks is born October 26 in Chicago, Illinois.

2002
CM Punk joins ROH.

2005
Punk wins the ROH world championship and then signs a contract with WWE.

2007
Punk pins John Morrison to win the ECW championship.

2008
The tag team of Punk and Kofi Kingston wins the world tag-team championship.

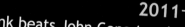

2009
Punk wins his second straight Money in the Bank match.

2011
Punk beats John Cena to win his first WWE championship.

2013
After holding the WWE title for more than a year, Punk finally loses the belt to the Rock.

GLOSSARY

backyard wrestling
A form of wrestling in which amateurs imitate professional wrestling matches.

finishing move
A powerful move that a wrestler uses to finish off an opponent.

Go to Sleep (GTS)
CM Punk's finishing move. Punk lifts an opponent above his head and then drops the opponent into Punk's knee.

heel
A wrestler whom fans view as a villain.

Money in the Bank match
A match between multiple wrestlers during which the goal is to grab a briefcase that hangs suspended from the ceiling.

rival
An opponent with whom one has an intense competition.

tap out
To surrender a match by tapping the mat.

INDEX